Taylor Swift
FOR FLUTE

ISBN 978-1-70519-266-5

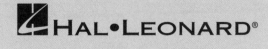

Visit Hal Leonard Online at
www.halleonard.com

World headquarters, contact:
Hal Leonard
7777 West Bluemound Road
Milwaukee, WI 53213
Email: info@halleonard.com

In Europe, contact:
Hal Leonard Europe Limited
1 Red Place
London, W1K 6PL
Email: info@halleonardeurope.com

In Australia, contact:
Hal Leonard Australia Pty. Ltd.
4 Lentara Court
Cheltenham, Victoria, 3192 Australia
Email: info@halleonard.com.au

ALL TOO WELL

Flute

Words and Music by TAYLOR SWIFT
and LIZ ROSE

ANTI-HERO

Flute

Words and Music by TAYLOR SWIFT
and JACK ANTONOFF

(small notes optional)

CHANGE

FLUTE

Words and Music by
TAYLOR SWIFT

BACK TO DECEMBER

Flute

Words and Music by
TAYLOR SWIFT

Moderately

To Coda

7

D.S. al Coda

CODA

BLANK SPACE

FLUTE

Words and Music by TAYLOR SWIFT,
MAX MARTIN and SHELLBACK

CARDIGAN

FLUTE

Words and Music by TAYLOR SWIFT
and AARON DESSNER

CHAMPAGNE PROBLEMS

FLUTE

Words and Music by TAYLOR SWIFT
and WILLIAM BOWERY

EVERMORE

FLUTE

Words and Music by TAYLOR SWIFT,
WILLIAM BOWERY and JUSTIN VERNON

EXILE

FLUTE

Words and Music by TAYLOR SWIFT,
WILLIAM BOWERY and JUSTIN VERNON

FEARLESS

Flute

Words and Music by TAYLOR SWIFT,
LIZ ROSE and HILLARY LINDSEY

FIFTEEN

FLUTE

Words and Music by
TAYLOR SWIFT

CODA

D.S. al Coda

I KNEW YOU WERE TROUBLE

Flute

Words and Music by TAYLOR SWIFT,
SHELLBACK and MAX MARTIN

LAVENDER HAZE

Flute

Words and Music by TAYLOR SWIFT,
ZOË KRAVITZ, JACK ANTONOFF,
MARK ANTHONY SPEARS,
SAM DEW and JAHAAN AKIL SWEET

LOVE STORY

FLUTE

Words and Music by
TAYLOR SWIFT

Moderately

27

MEAN

FLUTE

Words and Music by
TAYLOR SWIFT

MINE

FLUTE

Words and Music by
TAYLOR SWIFT

Moderately fast

THE 1

Flute

Words and Music by TAYLOR SWIFT
and AARON DESSNER

D.S. al Coda
(with repeat)

CODA

OUR SONG

FLUTE

Words and Music by
TAYLOR SWIFT

rit.

PICTURE TO BURN

FLUTE

Words and Music by TAYLOR SWIFT
and LIZ ROSE

SHAKE IT OFF

FLUTE

Words and Music by TAYLOR SWIFT,
MAX MARTIN and SHELLBACK

CODA

SHOULD'VE SAID NO

FLUTE

Words and Music by
TAYLOR SWIFT

SPARKS FLY

FLUTE

Words and Music by
TAYLOR SWIFT

SPEAK NOW

FLUTE

Words and Music by
TAYLOR SWIFT

SWEET NOTHING

Flute

Words and Music by TAYLOR SWIFT
and WILLAM BOWERY

TEARDROPS ON MY GUITAR

Flute

Words and Music by TAYLOR SWIFT
and LIZ ROSE

49

rit.

TODAY WAS A FAIRYTALE

FLUTE

Words and Music by
TAYLOR SWIFT

22

FLUTE

Words and Music by TAYLOR SWIFT,
SHELLBACK and MAX MARTIN

WE ARE NEVER EVER GETTING BACK TOGETHER

FLUTE

Words and Music by TAYLOR SWIFT,
MAX MARTIN and SHELLBACK

WHITE HORSE

Flute

Words and Music by TAYLOR SWIFT
and LIZ ROSE

rit.

WILLOW

Flute

Words and Music by TAYLOR SWIFT
and AARON DESSNER

D.C. al Coda
(no repeat)

CODA

YOU BELONG WITH ME

Flute

Words and Music by TAYLOR SWIFT
and LIZ ROSE

YOU NEED TO CALM DOWN

Flute

Words and Music by TAYLOR SWIFT
and JOEL LITTLE

(small notes optional)

LOOK WHAT YOU MADE ME DO

flute

Words and Music by TAYLOR SWIFT,
JACK ANTONOFF, RICHARD FAIRBRASS,
FRED FAIRBRASS and ROB MANZOLI